BORN TO SHOP © and ® 2006 History & Heraldry Ltd.
All rights reserved.

This edition published by Ravette Publishing 2006.

Printed and bound in Belgium

ISBN 10: 1-84161-256-1
ISBN 13: 978-1-84161-256-0

ЯR
RAVETTE PUBLISHING

Lead me not into temptation, I can find the way myself

I eat all the
main food groups,
microwave,
fast and
frozen

I'd give up cake, but I'm no quitter

Fridge pickers

wear

bigger

knickers

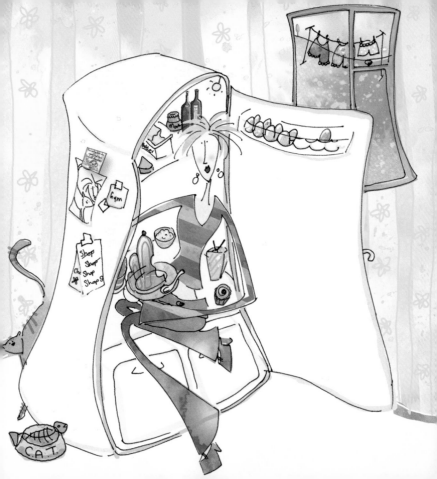

I'm on a
Gin and Tonic diet,
so far I've lost
two days

Save the Earth,
it's the only
planet with
chocolate

Never eat
more
than you can
lift

At Easter
size
does count

I keep trying
to lose weight,
but it keeps
finding me

If they don't
have cake
in heaven
I'm not
going!

Lord if you won't make me Skinny, please make my friends fat

There's nothing
better than a good
friend except
a good friend
with chocolate

I love to cook with wine, sometimes I even put it in the food

So much chocolate log, so little time

I take life with
a pinch of salt, a
wedge of lime
and a shot of
tequila

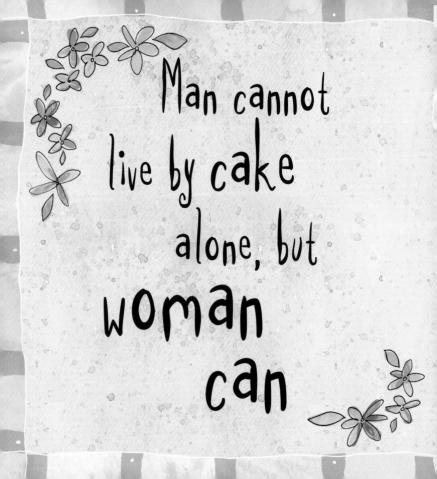

A balanced diet is a burger in each hand

Other BORN TO SHOP titles available ...

	ISBN	Price
Another day in paradise	1 84161 255 3	£4.99
Friends are the family we choose for ourselves	1 84161 254 5	£4.99
All men are created equal ... equally useless	1 84161 257 X	£4.99

HOW TO ORDER   Please send a cheque/postal order in £ sterling, made payable
to 'Ravette Publishing' for the cover price of the books and
allow the following for post & packaging ...

UK & BFPO   70p for the first book & 40p per book thereafter
Europe & Eire   £1.30 for the first book & 70p per book thereafter
Rest of the world £2.20 for the first book & £1.10 per book thereafter

RAVETTE PUBLISHING LTD
Unit 3 Tristar Centre
Star Road
Partridge Green
West Sussex RH13 8RA
Tel: 01403 711443   Fax: 01403 711554   Email: ravettepub@aol.com

Prices and availability are subject to change without prior notice.